Let's Read About... Martin Luther King, Jr.

Scholastic First Biographies™

by Courtney Baker

Illustrated by Cornelius Van Wright
and Ying-Hwa Hu

SCHOLASTIC INC. Cartwheel B·O·O·K·S ®

New York   Toronto   London   Auckland
Sydney   Mexico City   New Delhi   Hong Kong

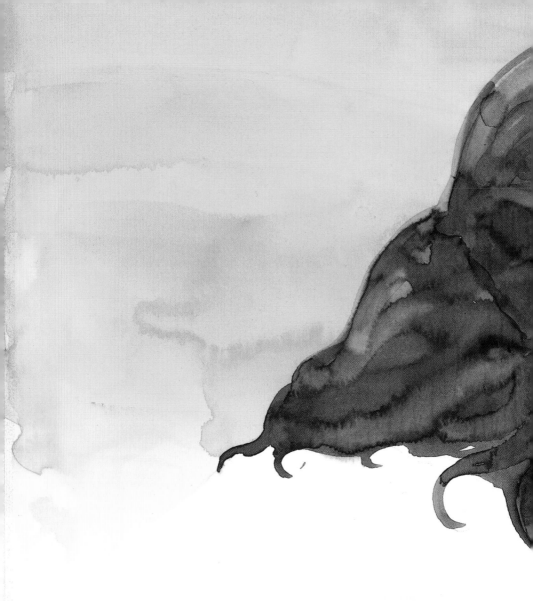

Martin Luther King, Jr., was born on
January 15, 1929, in Atlanta, Georgia.

He lived with his parents.
He had an older sister and a younger brother.

Martin's father was a minister.
Martin grew up listening
to his father speak in church.
The people at church
liked the way Martin's father spoke.
They sang and clapped.

Martin knew the people in church.
He lived near them.
He went to school with them.
He saw them on the street.

Sometimes, Martin went
to the city with his family.

He saw signs that said "Whites Only"
at the park and at the movies.

The signs meant that Martin and his
family could not go to those places.
Martin felt that black people should
be able to go to the same places
as white people.

When he was six, he had a friend
who was white.
They liked each other and played together.

But soon, the boy's parents said they did
not want their son to play with Martin
any longer.
Martin felt very bad.
He was sad that he had to stop playing
with his friend.

That day, Martin's mother told him, "You're as good as anyone else, and don't you forget it!"
Martin felt better.
He knew that the boy's parents did not really know him.
If they had, they would have seen how nice and smart Martin was!

When he was eight,
Martin worked as
a newspaper boy.
He was very good
at his job.

Martin used the money
he earned to buy books.
He read about people
who fought racism.

Racism is the idea that
people who are different
colors are not equal.
Martin thought that all
people were equal.
He wanted to fight racism, too.

Martin became a minister like his father.
Martin gave speeches and talked
about equality.
He traveled to speak to church groups
and to large crowds.

He spoke to a crowd of 250,000 people
in Washington, D.C.
He spoke about his dream for the future.
"I have a dream," Martin said,
"that my four little children
will one day live in a nation
where they will not be judged
by the color of their skin
but by the content
of their character."

Some people did not like what Martin was saying.

Most people did. Martin helped to change the way people thought and acted toward one another.

Today, many people remember his dream and try to make the world a better place for everyone.